Blessed with Extraordinary

Support and resources for families of children with Down Syndrome

Linda A. Bonner

Blessed with Extraordinary Workbook — Support and resources for families of children with Down Syndrome
Copyright © 2024 Linda Bonner

Published by:
Aviva Publishing
Lake Placid, NY
https://avivapubs.com

All inquiries:
Linda A. Bonner
www.lindabonnerstudios.com
lindabonnerstudios@gmail.com

ISBN: 978-1-63618-316-9 (Paperback)
Library of Congress Control Number: 2023910802

Editor: Jane Maulucci, The Active Voice
Cover design and interior layout: Yael Halpern, Y.Halpern Designs

Every attempt has been made to properly source all quotes

First printing edition 2024
Printed in the United States of America

10 9 8 7 6 5 4 3 2 1

Table of Contents

INTRODUCTION

Blessed with Extraordinary is my personal account, from a mother's perspective, of my journey to raise my son, Kevin, who has Down Syndrome. What I share in the book are my own personal feelings, emotions, and experiences. When Kevin was born, I was overwhelmed with first becoming a parent and second being the parent of a child who needed specific medical attention and therapies to meet his daily needs.

I designed and wrote the book for parents and caregivers of children with Down Syndrome to share the encouragement I received while raising my son. In my desperate search for information to be the best possible mom for Kevin, I met with and talked to anyone who could expand my base of knowledge.

Finding and accessing the resources I needed took a lot of work. It is my privilege to share what I,Äôve experienced and learned in an effort to help others on this incredible journey. I,Äôve been where you are, struggling with uncertainty.

I have created this companion workbook to become a ready resource for you that you can keep handy and pick up as you need it.

In this workbook, you'll have places to record important information from contact numbers for caregivers to self-care tips, from Life Care Planning for your child to the minor and major celebrations of raising a child with Down Syndrome.

This workbook is designed to serve and support you on your journey of loving, caring for, and growing with your child.

My heart goes with you,

Linda

Chapter 1

OFF TO A GOOD START

Every baby is an adjustment, and a child with Down Syndrome requires some extra considerations. Get started by reaching out to your local support services. Use these exercises to help you get off to a good start!

CONSIDER THIS	RESPONSE
What therapy services could your child benefit from right now? For example: Speech, physical, or occupational therapy.	
Who have you contacted for ECI (Early Childhood Intervention) for children birth to age 3 to get these services started? Record their contact information and notes from your conversations.	
Has your child experienced any medical condition beyond their primary diagnosis of Down Syndrome? Do you have the specialists you need? Where can you go for referrals?	
Begin to document your journey. You can create a handwritten account, a digital document, scrapbooks, or record events on a calendar so you can remember the milestones for your child. **Where will you keep your valuable memories?**	
What initial moments can you celebrate?	

Chapter 2

PRE-SCHOOL

Pre-school was a huge letting-go moment for me. Through some tears, I waved goodbye to my baby. I had just handed over the care and nurturing of my child to teachers and assistants who promised to teach him the skills he needed to go to kindergarten. We also got involved in other active therapies and Special Olympics. Use the exercises below to prepare yourself and your child for their pre-school years.

CONSIDER THIS	RESPONSE
How are you preparing yourself and your child for preschool?	
What therapy options have you pursued for your child? List the options and their contact information.	
Special Olympics is an option for children with a wide range of abilities. List the contact information for your local Special Olympics resource.	

Chapter 3

ELEMENTARY & MIDDLE SCHOOL

You are your child's best advocate. By being involved with their schooling, knowing their teachers, and establishing expectations and outcomes, you and your child will have a positive school experience. Use these prompts as a guide to advocacy for your child.

CONSIDER THIS	RESPONSE
How and when can you be an advocate for your child?	
Who was involved in creating your child's IEP/Individual Education Plan? What additional support do you need?	
Where have you stored the copy of your child's plan? Be sure to keep copies of all IEPs.	

Where can you, as a parent, take advantage of your rights to get the very best support and services for your child?	
How can you respond when you feel your child is being treated differently due to having Down Syndrome?	
Who can you contact to support you?	

Chapter 4

OUTSIDE ACTIVITIES

Whether your child is interested in sports, art, or theater, find a way for them to participate outside their daily routine. Research various classes and programs and ask if they can accommodate your child's needs. Use this exercise to note your child's interests and possible activities they can participate in.

CONSIDER THIS	RESPONSE
What emerging interests have you noticed in your child? Begin researching those areas for classes, groups, or activities they can join to encourage those interests.	
Who do you know (other children, family members, or friends) who could include your child in play or recreation activities to expand their options?	

Chapter 5

HIGH SCHOOL

High school is an exciting time for your child. They are becoming more independent, connecting with more people, and ready to consider entering the workforce with a part-time job. Use these prompts to envision the high school experience for you and your child.

CONSIDER THIS	RESPONSE
Even if your child isn't at this stage yet, begin thinking about the outcomes you'd like to see in high school. Make a list of priorities for your child with their input if they are nearing or in high school.	
What type of job environments might be a good fit for your child based on their interests?	
Who can support you and your child with their high school journey?	

Chapter 6

POST HIGH SCHOOL

Your child's educational opportunities do not end with high school. There are many options for post-secondary education, including degree programs and technical or trade schools. This is also the time when you and your child need to consider their independent living options. Use these prompts to start the post-high school planning process.

CONSIDER THIS	RESPONSE
Research local post-secondary programs in your area. What does your school district offer?	
What types of independent living facilities are available in your area for your child?	
Where can you connect with other parents of post-high school children in your community?	

Chapter 7

INDEPENDENT LIVING SKILLS

Independent living skills are the skills that every person utilizes on a daily basis to live on their own. These include self-care skills such as eating, dressing, bathing, toileting, and grooming. Other skills that come under the heading of home management are cleaning, shopping, laundry, money management, medication management, and time management, among others. Teaching independent living skills to any child is a process that begins at birth and goes on until adulthood. Use this prompt to record the skills your child needs now and in the future and the resources you can use.

CONSIDER THIS	RESPONSE
Determine which independence skills your child is ready for, and start a prioritized list that you can begin working on. Contact a local speech, occupational, or physical therapist for a list of skills.	
What type of outside help do you need? For example, a coach or therapist.	

Chapter **8**

FAITH & GRATITUDE

On my journey to healing and acceptance, I learned the importance of building a strong foundation of faith. When nothing else worked and times were difficult, my faith was what helped me through. There are many types of faith, and for you, it might be faith in yourself or your abilities or something else greater than yourself. Use these prompts to connect and build your inner guidance system.

CONSIDER THIS	RESPONSE
What does your faith look like? Spend time reflecting and journaling on what faith means to you.	
What helps you to find your inner peace and strength? List a few of the inspirations you rely on and post them in prominent places where you can frequently be reminded.	
Gratitude has been shown to be a wondrous tool for building inner peace. Design your daily gratitude practice.	

Chapter 9

SELF-CARE & CAREGIVER BILL OF RIGHTS

Self-care is often easier said than done. As a parent, I put my child first, which left little time or energy to invest in myself. I probably don't have to tell you that if we don‚Äôt take care of ourselves, we become emotionally and physically exhausted parents, which isn‚Äôt what our children need. Use these prompts to ensure that you put self-care as a priority.

CONSIDER THIS	RESPONSE
SELF-CARE	
List your current self-care activities in each category.	Physical
	Psychological
	Emotional
	Spiritual
What can you add to your self-care routine at this point in your caregiving journey?	

TAKE A BREAK

What does it mean for you to take a break? Journal about some of the things you used to enjoy and consider how you can build them, or some variation, back into your routine.

AFFIRMATIONS	
Counteract your feelings of guilt, unworthiness, and negativity by journaling about them and then write out positive statements to help you overcome those emotions.	
Research and record affirmations that are important and relevant to your life. Remember to read them often and build on your list as your life changes.	
CAREGIVER BILL OF RIGHTS	
What caregiving rights do you need to identify and document? Write out your needs, wants, and expectations.	
Where do you need to set boundaries to protect your privacy, needs, and wants?	

Chapter 10

FINDING SUPPORT

When my child with Down Syndrome was born, my first instinct was to isolate myself. Like other events in my life, I thought I had to figure this out on my own because no one could possibly understand how I felt or what I was going through. I then learned that there were many people and organizations that were able to assist me if I just asked! Use these prompts to remind yourself that you are not alone on this journey and that there are other people ready, willing, and able to help you.

CONSIDER THIS	RESPONSE
Which areas in your life could you use some assistance? For instance: Personal/Emotional Support Caring for your child Financial Guidance Household Maintenance Time Management	
What resources are available to you within your community or family?	

Chapter 11

THE SMALL THINGS ARE WORTH CELEBRATING

Life is a series of significant little moments. These small moments are what make life more memorable. For you and your child, these incremental victories deserve to be recognized, acknowledged, and celebrated! By celebrating what seems like a tiny milestone, you will experience more happiness and motivation, and your child will gain confidence through your encouragement. Use these prompts to encourage yourself to celebrate often and to record your joy.

CONSIDER THIS	RESPONSE
How will you record and celebrate the little moments in your child's life? Photos Video Victory Journal	
What recent moments do you recall that you can document and celebrate?	
What are you grateful for at this moment?	

Chapter 12

LIFE CARE PLANNING & LEGAL NEEDS

According to the Special Needs Alliance, a Life Care Plan is "...a blueprint for providing the economic security and services that someone with special needs will require in order to live a fulfilling life, as independently as possible." Use these prompts to help build a Life Care Plan for your child.

CONSIDER THIS	RESPONSE
What desires and expectations do you have for your child? Begin documenting them.	
Research the "All About" document in the resources section. What can you start documenting today about your child that can help with future planning?	
Create a list of the information you will need to prepare a *Letter of Intent* **and start gathering it.**	

Where is your will maintained? If you don't already have one, locate a licensed attorney that specializes in disability law. Make note of your contacts and any questions you have for your attorney.	
If your child is 16, begin researching guardianship vs. supported decision-making. Which path is best for your child and your family?	
Before your child turns 18, begin the process of applying for Medicaid as well as SSI/SSDI. Note your contacts and research all your options.	

ALL ABOUT ME!

This document is lovingly prepared to provide any caregiver with vital information about your loved one. It contains detailed medical information, simple likes and dislikes, a daily schedule to maintain continuity, key contacts, and personal information that will make life easier and more enjoyable for both the caregiver and your child.

Name:	Birthdate:

Nickname:

Diagnosis:

Medical Devices:
Such as implants, hearing aids, assistive devices, medical bracelets, etc.

CURRENT PRESCRIBED AND OVER-THE-COUNTER MEDICATIONS				
Medication	Dosage	Schedule / Time Taken	Purpose	Prescriber

DAILY LIVING SKILLS
What are your loved one's abilities or challenges? Be specific. What can they do on their own?
What skills do they need assistance with and how much?

Height/Weight:	Shirt Size:
Pant Size:	Shoe Size:

DIETARY INFORMATION

Food Allergies:

Food Preferences:

Food Dislikes:

FAMILY & FRIENDS

List any contact that your loved one currently has contact with or has had a special relationship in the past. Include family members, respite providers, teachers, therapists, friends, other parents, and other people who are important to their life.

Name	Relationship	Contact

DAILY ACTIVITIES, MONDAY–SUNDAY:

List anything someone would need to know about your loved one's routine. Be as detailed as possible.

MEAL TIMES	Breakfast	Lunch	Snack	Dinner

Shower/Bath Time:	
Bed Time:	Nap Time:
Exercise/PT Time:	Play Time:

DAILY SCHEDULE

MONDAY

Morning

Afternoon

Evening

TUESDAY

Morning

Afternoon

Evening

WEDNESDAY
Morning
Afternoon
Evening

THURSDAY
Morning
Afternoon
Evening

FRIDAY
Morning
Afternoon
Evening

SATURDAY
Morning
Afternoon
Evening

SUNDAY
Morning
Afternoon
Evening

FAVORITE ACTIVITIES
List sports, adventures, movie, game, and book preferences, special places, and best down time activities.

SCHEDULED ACTIVITIES
List each activity/program, including contact info and name, time and day of activity, and other details.

Therapy

Employment

Social/Clubs

School/Community

MEDICAL PROVIDERS
List the name, address, and contact information for each provider. Include most recent appointments and frequency of visit.

Primary Care

Specialists

Dentist

Eye Doctor

IMMUNIZATIONS: List current immunizations.

    Tetanus

    Covid

    Flu

    Other

GOVERNMENT BENEFITS & LEGALITIES
Include contact numbers and resource information.

Social Security/SSDI/SSI

Medicaid

Guardianship

Family Attorney

Resource Guide

This is not intended as an exhaustive list of resources for the IDD community. It is designed to provide a starting point for topics related to people with Down Syndrome and to enhance your personal research. Inclusion of these resources does not constitute an endorsement of their products or services.

Down Syndrome Organizations

NDDS: National Down Syndrome Congress

The National Down Syndrome Congress (NDSC) is a not-for-profit organization dedicated to an improved world for individuals with Down syndrome. Founded in 1973, we are the leading national resource of support and information for anyone touched by or seeking to learn about Down syndrome, from the moment of diagnosis, whether prenatal or at birth, through adulthood.

www.ndsccenter.org

NDSS: National Down Syndrome Society

NDSS empowers individuals with Down syndrome and their families by driving policy change, providing resources, engaging with local communities, and shifting public perceptions.

www.ndss.org

NADS: National Association for Down Syndrome

NADS was founded in 1961 in Chicago and is the oldest organization in the country serving individuals with Down Syndrome and their families. Their mission is to support all people with Down Syndrome in achieving their full potential.

www.nads.org

Global Down Syndrome Foundation

The Global Down Syndrome Foundation is a public non-profit 501(c)(3) dedicated to significantly improving the lives of people with Down Syndrome through research, medical care, education, and advocacy.

www.globaldownsyndrome.org

Important Down Syndrome Events

World Down Syndrome Day (WDSD) – March 21

WDSD is a global awareness day that has been recognized by the United Nations since 2012. The date for WDSD, being the 21st day of the 3rd month, was selected to signify the uniqueness of the triplication (trisomy) of the 21st chromosome, which causes Down syndrome.

Down Syndrome Awareness Month – October

October was first designated as Down Syndrome Awareness Month in the 1980s and has been recognized every year since then. It's a time to celebrate people with Down Syndrome and make others aware of their abilities and accomplishments.

Down Syndrome Support Services

Resources for your Infant with Disabilities
- Early childhood Intervention: Services for children from birth to 3 with disabilities
  Search for "Early Childhood Intervention [YOUR STATE]"
- Local Government Resources & Support
  Search "Local IDD Authority [YOUR STATE]"

Parent to Parent USA
Their mission is to support a national network of Parent to Parent programs to ensure access to quality emotional support for families of individuals with disabilities and/or special health care needs. They offer parent mentors, education, and support for families of children with disabilities.

www.p2pusa.org
Search www.p2p[STATE].org

Building a Personal Network
- https://www.navigatelifetexas.org/en/blog/article/personal-networks-building-relationships-for-the-long-haul
- https://www.txp2p.org/services/texas-network-connections
- https://www.txp2p.org/Media/Transition/network_resources.pdf
- https://plan.ca/

Special Olympics
Special Olympics athletes are eight years old or older and have intellectual or developmental disabilities. There is no upper age limit, and in fact, nearly one-third of Special Olympics athletes are aged 22 or older.

https://www.specialolympics.org/get-involved/athlete

Letter of Intent / Life Care Planning Template
https://thearc.org/resource/letter-of-intent/
https://www.bridges4kids.org/letter-of-intent-form.pdf

10 Disability Organizations You Should Know About
https://www.friendshipcircle.org/blog/2016/01/14/10-special-needs-organizations-you-should-know-about/

Yellow Pages for Kids with Disabilities
Find educational consultants, psychologists, educational diagnosticians, health care providers, academic

therapists, tutors, speech-language therapists, occupational therapists, coaches, advocates, and attorneys for children with disabilities.

https://www.yellowpagesforkids.com

Independence Skills

https://www.osfhealthcare.org/blog/how-to-encourage-your-child-with-special-needs/

https://www.brighthubeducation.com/special-ed-inclusion-strategies/71939-teaching-independent-living-skills/

https://www.pediaplex.net/blog/encouraging-independence-for-children-with-special-needs

My Steps To: Window Cards to Teach Independence Skills

https://www.etsy.com/shop/mystepsto

Adaptive Recreation

Leisure activities such as animal-assisted therapy, recreational drumming, adaptive sports, and other recreational programs that help with reducing anxiety, improving social skills and the overall quality of life.

https://www.friendshipcircle.org/blog/2015/01/28/10-types-of-recreational-therapy-to-help-your-childreach-your-goals/

https://www.nctrc.org/about-ncrtc/about-recreational-therapy/

https://www.recrespite.com/using-recreation-therapy-to-promote-inclusion-and-active-participation/

Education Support

IDEA: Individuals with Disabilities Education Act

The Individuals with Disabilities Education Act (IDEA) is a law that makes available **Free Appropriate Public Education** (FAPE) to eligible children with disabilities throughout the nation and ensures special education and related services to those children.

https://sites.ed.gov/idea/

ECSE: Early Childhood Special Education

Public-school program for young children, ages 3-5, with disabilities

Search Early Childhood Special Education [your state]

https://www.aacap.org/aacap/families_and_youth/facts_for_families/fff-guide/Services-In-School-For-Children-With-Special-Needs-What-Parents-Need-To-Know-083.aspx

Local Special Education School Services

Search Special Education Services [STATE]

Special Education Advocates

https://www.p2pusa.org/

https://www.navigatelifetexas.org/en/education-schools/special-education-advocates-and-advocacy https://www.understood.org/en/articles/how-to-find-a-special-education-advocate

Search "Special Education Advocates near me"

https://www.parentingspecialneeds.org/article/advocating-for-your-child/

Person Centered Planning

https://www.pacer.org/transition/learning-center/independent-community-living/person-centered.asp

https://acl.gov/programs/consumer-control/person-centered-planning

Special Olympics in Schools

Many school districts offer Special Olympics events for pre-K through age 21. Check with your local school district for more information.

Advocacy

https://ldaamerica.org/advocacy/what-is-advocacy/

https://ldaamerica.org/info/general-tips-on-advocacy-by-parents/

https://www.wrightslaw.com/

Personal Support

Self-Care Resources

https://www.waterford.org/education/self-care-for-parents/

https://www.verywellfamily.com/

https://www.goodtherapy.org/blog/self-care-tips-for-parents-of-special-needs-children

https://themighty.com/topic/general-parenting/self-care-parent-child-disabilities

https://soundgirls.org/self-care-develop-a-routine-that-works-for-you/

https://www.odvn.org/wp-content/uploads/2020/05/50-ways-to-take-a-break-printable.pdf

Affirmations

Statements of positive self-talk

https://www.familyaware.org/10-empowering-self-affirmations-for-the-family-caregiver/

Caregiver's Bill of Rights

https://www.caregiver.org/resource/caregivers-bill-rights/

https://www.parentcompanion.org/article/parent-and-caregiver-bill-of-rights

https://www.usa.gov/disability-caregiver

The Power of Gratitude

https://www.psychologytoday.com/us/blog/compassion-matters/201511/the-healing-power-gratitude

Meetup Groups

Meetup is a social networking site that allows you to find and join groups related to your own personal interests, such as your child's disability.

www.meetup.com/

Support Groups

The Arc promotes and protects the human rights of people with intellectual and developmental disabilities and actively supports their full inclusion and participation in the community throughout their lifetimes.

https://thearc.org/find-a-chapter/

Parent 2 Parent USA provides empowerment and support for parents or families of children and loved ones with disabilities.

https://www.p2pusa.org/

Down Syndrome Guild [YOUR CITY].

Local Support Groups. [DISABILITY] Support Group {YOUR CITY].

Counseling, Therapy, Life Coaching

https://www.regain.us/advice/counseling/counseling-vs-therapy-what-are-the-differences-and-which-option-is-best-for-you/

https://www.entrepreneur.com/article/347144

Counseling vs. Life Coaching

Meal Train

Organized meal giving around significant life events.

https://www.mealtrain.com/

Government Agency Support Services

SSI/SSDI –

Social Security Disability Insurance (SSDI) and Supplemental Security Income (SSI)

https://www.ssa.gov/disability/

Americans With Disabilities Act – ADA

Protecting people with disabilities from discrimination.

https://www.ada.gov/

Disability Resources from the Department of Labor

https://www.dol.gov/odep/topics/disability.htm

SNAP – Supplemental Nutrition Assistance Program

https://www.fns.usda.gov/snap/supplemental-nutrition-assistance-program

Programs for People with Disabilities

https://www.hhs.gov/programs/social-services/programs-for-people-with-disabilities/index.html

Medicaid Waiver Programs by State

https://www.medicaid.gov/medicaid/section-1115-demo/demonstration-and-waiver-list/index.html

Health & Human Services

Guidance for CMS (Centers for Medicare & Medicaid Services) partnership with national organizations to ensure that persons with disabilities and chronic diseases receive access to quality health insurance and health care information.

https://www.hhs.gov/guidance/document/disability-organizations-coalitions-0

Aging and Disability Services

Aging and Disability Resource Centers (ADRCs) across the country seek to address the frustrations many older adults, people with disabilities, and family members experience when trying to learn about and access long-term services and support.

https://acl.gov/programs/aging-and-disability-networks

AAIDD - American Association on Intellectual & Developmental Disabilities

AAIDD is the oldest, largest, and most influential membership organization concerned with intellectual and developmental disabilities. Join the AAIDD community.

www.aaidd.org

Nationwide Disability Programs

https://www.disability.gov/

Family and Protective Services

Investigates charges of abuse, neglect or exploitation of children, elderly adults, and adults with disabilities.

Search [Your State] Family and Protective Services.

Legal Support

Guardianship and Supported Decision Making
Search "Guardianship" [STATE}
Search "Supported Decision Making" [STATE]

Legal Disability Rights
https://www.usa.gov/disability-rights

Legal Resources for People with Disabilities
https://www.justgreatlawyers.com/legal-resources-considerations-seniors-special-needs

Special Needs Trusts
Set aside money without affecting federal or state benefits.
Search "Special Needs Trust" [STATE]

Wills
Legal document to ensure your child is taken care of if you are no longer able to provide care.
Search for an attorney who specializes in disability law.